This recipe booklet belon

Introduction

This booklet is a collection of favorite recipes from our Food Smarts workshops and our EatFresh.org website. Most are simple one pot/pan/bowl dishes that don't require a lot of equipment. Many can be prepared without a full kitchen. You can also cut the recipe in half to make it for fewer people, or double it for a larger group.

If you need help, head to EatFresh.org on your computer, phone, or tablet and search for the recipe. There you can adjust serving sizes, find ingredient substitutions, learn how to shop for fruits and vegetables, get tips on healthy eating, find new recipes, and more!

nutrition pantry program

food smarts

eatFresh

Contents

See page 9 for icon descriptions.

Getting Ready

Cooking Terms

	Method	Temperature	Time	Notes
Dry Heat	Bake			Food is surrounded by heat to cook.
	Broil			Food is cooked by direct exposure to very high heat.
	Deep Fry			Food is cooked in a deep layer of very hot oil.
	Fry			Food is cooked in a shallow layer of very hot oil.
	Grill			Food is cooked over direct heat.
	Roast			To brown and cook vegetables, meats, and fruits.
	Sauté			To cook/brown food in a little bit of fat (oil or butter).
Moist Heat	Boil			Liquid is heated until surface bubbles continuously
	Simmer			Food is heated slowly, with bubbles barely forming on the surface.
	Steam			To cook with steam from boiling water; usually covered.

Preparation Terms

Chop: to cut into bite-sized pieces.

Cube: to chop into cubes with straight edges.

Dice: to cut the food into smaller pieces, about ¼" pieces or cubes. *Dicing vegetables into small pieces allows for a quicker cooking time.*

Grate: to rub food on a grater to make shreds.

Julienne: to cut food into thin strips.

Knead: to press dough (i.e. for bread) repeatedly with hands.

Marinate: to pre-mix food with wet or dry seasonings. *This helps develop the flavor as well as moisturize it.*

Mince: to chop into extremely small pieces (the smallest possible dice). *For example, we mince garlic so no one gets a big chunk.*

Peel: to remove the skin of fruits or vegetables.

Puree: to blend until smooth.

Slice: to cut into flat, thin pieces.

Whip/whisk: to beat quickly, in order to add air and volume to food.

▊ Abbreviations Used

c. = cup   **tbsp.** = tablespoon   **tsp.** = teaspoon

lb. = pound   **oz.** = ounce

▊ Icons Used

Throughout this booklet, the following icons are used to indicate the cooking method(s) possible for each recipe.

 Stove top    Microwave   Oven

 Slow cooker   Rice cooker   No-cook

How to Read a Recipe

▌ What can go wrong if you don't read a recipe well?

It's easy to miss details in a recipe. Perhaps you invent something new... or have to throw out your dinner!

Smoothies

Prep Time: 5 min   **Yield:** 2

Cook Time: 0 min   **Serving Size:** 1 cup

Ingredients:
- » 4 frozen strawberries
- » 1 cup low-fat plain yogurt
- » ½ cup 100% orange juice
- » 1 banana, cut into chunks
- » 4 ice cubes

Directions:
- » Place all ingredients in a blender.
- » Cover and process until smooth.

Nutrition Facts:
150 calories, 2g total fat (1g sat), 30g carb, 2g fiber, 65mg sodium

1. Read the recipe well before starting.

    »   Make sure you have all the items you need, and enough time for the recipe.

    »   Look for any terms you don't know; see pages 8-9.

    »   When an ingredient is optional, you don't have to use it unless you want to.

    »   If necessary, preheat the oven while you prepare.

2. Prepare ingredients for the recipe.

    »   If a recipe calls for chopped onion, for example, do the chopping now. You might also need to bring ingredients to room temperature, melt them, or chill them before starting.

    »   To learn about ingredient substitutions, check EatFresh. org.

3. Measure carefully.

    »   It helps to know abbreviations: **c.** = cup, **T.** or **tbsp**. = tablespoon, **t.** or **tsp**. = teaspoon. It's also helpful to know measurement shortcuts. For example:

        »   4 tablespoons = ¼ cup

        »   3 teaspoons = 1 tablespoon

        »   1 cup liquid (volume) = 8 oz.

        »   1 pound (weight) = 16 oz.

4. Follow the steps in order!

5. If you make any changes to your recipe as you cook, make a note. That way you can prepare the dish exactly the same way next time—or not!

Food Safety

Follow these steps for a safer kitchen.

1. Food preparation surfaces (cutting boards, etc.) are breeding grounds for bacteria. If you use a cutting board and knife to cut raw meat, fish, or poultry, be sure to both clean and sanitize the surface before using it again.

2. Cook foods thoroughly. When meat is exposed to air, bacteria immediately begin to develop. To be safe, invest in a meat thermometer and test the meat for doneness. See chart on the following page.

3. Store raw meat and uncooked food on a lower shelf of your refrigerator. Also, keep eggs off the door and near the back, where temperatures remain the coldest. Your refrigerator should be kept at less than 40°F.

4. Once food is cooked, it should not sit out for more than four hours without being eaten or refrigerated.

5. It is never safe to leave frozen meat out on the countertop to defrost. **There are three ways to safely defrost foods:**

   » overnight in the refrigerator;
   » in a bowl of cold water, with the water changed every 30 minutes;
   » in the microwave; or
   » during cooking.

6. To ensure you have clean hands, wash them in hot, soapy water for at least 20 seconds. Sing the ABCs with kids to make it easy to wash effectively.

7. When you wash dishes, either use a dishwashing machine or wash them in the sink and allow them to air dry.

Cooking Temperature Chart

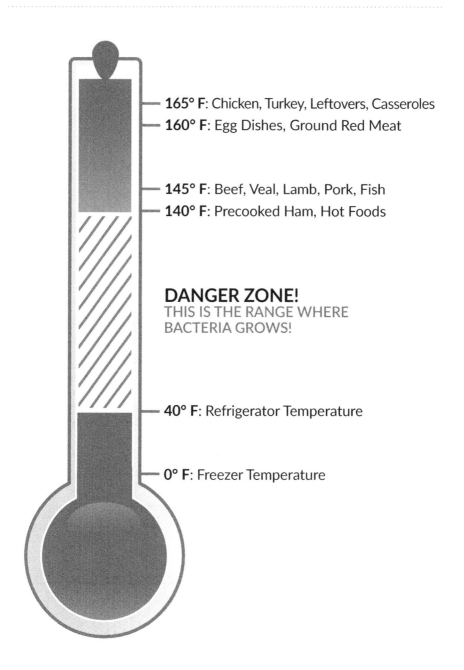

165° F: Chicken, Turkey, Leftovers, Casseroles
160° F: Egg Dishes, Ground Red Meat

145° F: Beef, Veal, Lamb, Pork, Fish
140° F: Precooked Ham, Hot Foods

DANGER ZONE!
THIS IS THE RANGE WHERE
BACTERIA GROWS!

40° F: Refrigerator Temperature

0° F: Freezer Temperature

Fruit and Vegetable Storage

» Some fruits and vegetables should be stored on the countertop to enable ripening and to ensure a better taste and texture. Take them out of their bags, unless you would like to speed the ripening process.

» Other produce will keep for much longer when stored in the refrigerator in a plastic bag with holes.

» Throw produce away if you see mold (usually white or brown) or if it has an "off" smell.

» Delicate produce such as lettuce and ripe peaches should be eaten within a few days, but heartier produce like onions, winter squash, and potatoes can be stored for over a month.

▮ Store at Room Temperature

» **Fruit:** apples, bananas, grapefruit, lemons, limes, oranges, mangoes, persimmons, whole pineapples, plantains, pomegranates, watermelons, peaches, pears, and plums.

» **Vegetables:** basil (with stems in water), onions, garlic, ginger, jicama, potatoes (keep from light to prevent greening), winter squashes and pumpkins, sweet potatoes, avocados, and tomatoes.

DID YOU KNOW? Fruits and veggies tend to fall into one of two categories: vapors or wilters. *Vapors* are those that emit as gas called ethylene that helps them ripen faster. *Wilters*, on the other hand, are highly susceptible to ethylene, which can cause them to go bad quickly. So, **it's best to store vapors and wilters separately.**

» Vapors include avocados, bananas, melons, potatoes, tomatoes, apples, ripe kiwis and peaches, and citrus.

» Wilters include broccoli, strawberries, carrots, garlic, eggplant, leafy greens, cucumbers, squash, and onions.

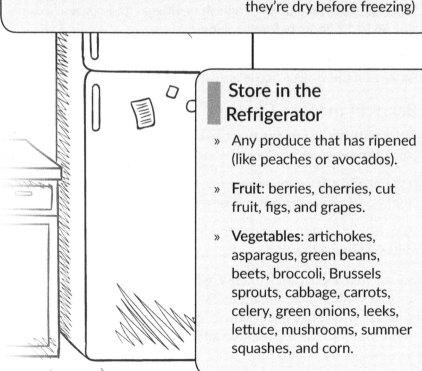

Long Term Freezer Storage

» Cut fresh fruit for baking, smoothies, and sauces

» Cooked fruits, vegetables, and herbs (make sure they're dry before freezing)

Store in the Refrigerator

» Any produce that has ripened (like peaches or avocados).

» **Fruit:** berries, cherries, cut fruit, figs, and grapes.

» **Vegetables:** artichokes, asparagus, green beans, beets, broccoli, Brussels sprouts, cabbage, carrots, celery, green onions, leeks, lettuce, mushrooms, summer squashes, and corn.

Using a Rice Cooker

A rice cooker is an electric pot that uses medium heat to steam food. It works faster than a slow cooker. (Time: 20-60 minutes)

Other characteristics include:

» shuts off automatically

» safer than stove top cooking because it has no exposed heat source

» inexpensive

Rice cookers are great for: *grain or bean dishes, soups, stews, curries, and steamed foods.*

Grains in the Rice Cooker

» Cook more than just rice in your rice cooker! Rice, millet, barley, quinoa, wheat berries, polenta, oats, and couscous are all good options. Soak grains with a splash of vinegar (to improve texture) for up to 12 hours before cooking.

» Use a little less water than you would usually when you cook the grains on the stove since less evaporates in the rice cooker.

Beans in the Rice Cooker

» Stick with smaller beans that cook more quickly, or make sure to soak the larger, more-dense beans before cooking.

» Do not add salt or anything acidic (such as lemon juice and tomatoes), or your beans will take longer to cook.

» Beans that can be cooked without soaking are lentils, split peas, and split mung beans.

» Beans that should soak for at least 12 hours before being cooked include pinto, black, kidney, and white. For these beans, check them after one rice cooker cycle. If they're still not done, add more water to the top and run another cycle until they're soft.

Complete Meals in a Rice Cooker

» A rice cooker can be used to prepare a one "pot" meal by piling vegetables and proteins into the rice cooker along with various grains.

» Since some components take longer to cook, you'll need to think about matching your ingredients that cook for about the same time (or chop up veggies into smaller pieces if they're heartier – like potatoes and onions).

» If you like your veggies crunchy, add them toward the end of cooking.

Chicken, Rice, and Vegetables (page 45) and Quinoa, Chickpeas, and Greens (page 46) are two recipes you can make entirely in a rice cooker.

Breakfast in a Rice Cooker

» Make soft-, medium-, or hard-cooked eggs in a rice cooker! Pour about two cups of water in the rice cooker pan, then place the eggs in the steamer basket and cover. Steam the eggs for about 20-30 minutes, depending on your preference.

» Make scrambled eggs! Put a tablespoon of oil or butter in the bottom of the rice cooker pan and turn the cooker on. Break eggs into the pan and stir every few minutes until the eggs are cooked completely through (about 15-20 minutes for 1-2 eggs). For an easy omelet, add mix-ins like meat, cheese, and veggies before adding the eggs.

» Make oatmeal! Add all the ingredients to your rice cooker bowl before turning it on for one cycle. (If using steel cut oats, use two cycles.) Try Pumpkin Oatmeal (page 25) this way.

» Even pancakes?! Yes, you can. See the recipe for Whole Wheat Pancakes on page 24.

Using a Slow Cooker (Crockpot)

A slow cooker, or crockpot, is an electric pot that uses very low heat to cook food slowly. (Time: 4-10 hours)

Common slow cooker characteristics include:

» has no exposed heat source and does not get hot enough to burn food

» can be left alone for hours

» uses less energy than many other appliances

» inexpensive

Slow cookers are great for: *soups, stews, tough meat, and dried beans.*

▌Slow Cooker Basics

» For most slow cookers, the LOW setting is about 200°F, and the HIGH setting is about 300°F.

» One hour on HIGH is equal to two hours on LOW.

» Fill the slow cooker one half to two thirds full so that the food does not cook too quickly or too slowly.

» Liquids do not boil away in the slow cooker, so if you are making a recipe that wasn't specifically developed for the slow cooker, reduce the liquid by 1/3 to 1/2 (unless you are cooking rice or making soup).

» The ceramic insert in a slow cooker can crack if exposed to abrupt temperature shifts. Always put a dish towel on the counter before putting down the hot ceramic insert. Similarly, don't put a ceramic insert straight from the refrigerator into a preheated base.

 Easy Meatballs and Sauce (page 38) and Turkey Rice Soup with Ginger (page 49) are two recipes you can make entirely in a slow cooker.

Food Safety

» Cook on HIGH for the first hour to bring the temperature up to 165°F as quickly as possible.

» Defrost frozen foods before putting them in the slow cooker in order to cook the food at a safe temperature.

» Don't use whole chickens or roasts; cut the meat into chunks to ensure thorough cooking.

» Remove cooked food from the slow cooker before you refrigerate the food in order to cool it more quickly.

Slow Cooker Tips

» Fat retains heat better than water, so fattier foods like meat, will cook faster than less fatty foods, like vegetables. For more even cooking, trim excess fat off of meats.

» If you're cooking a dish with both meat and vegetables, place the vegetables on the bottom and sides of the insert and put the meat on top.

» Most meats require 8 hours of cooking on LOW. Cheaper cuts of meat are perfect for slow cooking since they become tender after hours of cooking.

» Don't lift the lid to stir or else you will need to extend the cooking time by at least 20 minutes. Stirring is usually not necessary.

» Add tender vegetables like tomatoes, mushrooms, and zucchini during the last 45 minutes of cooking time so they don't overcook. Add leafy greens even closer to the end of cooking.

» Stir in spices for the last hour of cooking in order to prevent them from losing flavor.

» Dairy products, like sour cream, milk, or yogurt, tend to break down in the slow cooker. To prevent this, add them during the last 15 minutes of cooking.

Using a Microwave Oven

A microwave cooks food very quickly using waves of energy and is great for small spaces. (Time: a few minutes) Power and cooking times vary among microwaves.

Microwaves are great for: *thawing frozen foods, ready-to-heat foods, hot beverages, and steamed rice or vegetables.* For example, using a microwave to steam food from the inside out helps retain more vitamins and minerals than just about any other cooking method!

■ Microwave Tips

» Make a single serving of popcorn in a microwave simply by placing ¼ cup of kernels into a brown paper lunch bag. Press the sides of the bag together at the top and fold down three times. Depending on the power of your microwave, turn it on for 2-4 minutes. Listen for the time between pops to slow to about 2 seconds and remove from the microwave. (Be careful opening the bag as hot steam will be released.)

» Cooking corn on the cob in the microwave is fast and easy! Place the corn—with the husk still on!—in the center of your microwave and turn it on for about three minutes, depending on the power of your microwave. Allow the corn to rest for a few minutes (until the outside is cool enough to handle) before removing the husk.

» Microwaves are also great for cooking a wide variety of egg dishes, from poached to scrambled, and more! Don't miss the recipe for One Mug Omelets on page 26.

» It's easy to toast coconut, seeds, or nuts in a microwave. Place the food in a single layer on a microwave-safe dish, then cook in 30- to 60-second bursts while stirring at each break, until the items reach their desired crunch.

Avocado, Rice, and Beans (page 36) and Fruit Crisp (page 66) are two recipes you can make entirely in a microwave.

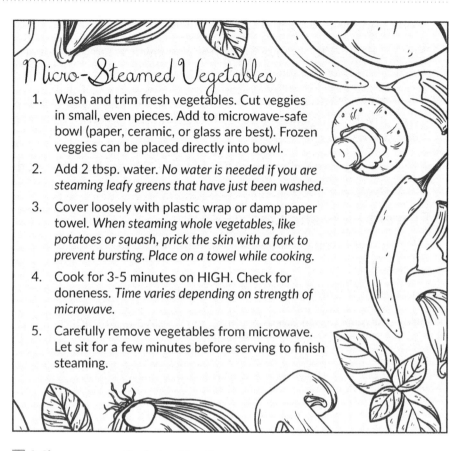

Micro-Steamed Vegetables

1. Wash and trim fresh vegetables. Cut veggies in small, even pieces. Add to microwave-safe bowl (paper, ceramic, or glass are best). Frozen veggies can be placed directly into bowl.

2. Add 2 tbsp. water. *No water is needed if you are steaming leafy greens that have just been washed.*

3. Cover loosely with plastic wrap or damp paper towel. *When steaming whole vegetables, like potatoes or squash, prick the skin with a fork to prevent bursting. Place on a towel while cooking.*

4. Cook for 3-5 minutes on HIGH. Check for doneness. *Time varies depending on strength of microwave.*

5. Carefully remove vegetables from microwave. Let sit for a few minutes before serving to finish steaming.

Microwave Safety Basics

» Read and follow microwave instructions on the package.

» Metal will make sparks in a microwave, so don't put tin foil, metal utensils, or food inside a stapled bag into your microwave.

» Do not turn on the microwave when there is nothing in it. Don't use it to heat or dry non-foods such as rags or clothing.

» Most plastic melts in a microwave. Use microwave-safe cookware; avoid microwaving in plastic, especially if not labeled *microwave-safe.*

» Foods like whole potatoes, hot dogs, and eggs will over heat and explode if you cook them too long. Poke holes in foods or microwave safe packages to avoid explosions.

» Lightly cover foods with microwave-safe plastic wrap, paper towels, or a plastic food cover designed for that purpose.

» Wipe up spills and clean the seal regularly.

» Use potholders to remove foods from the microwave oven. Keep potholders near the microwave.

» Boiling liquids can spill over in their cups and burn you. To prevent a spill, avoid filling cups or bowls more than halfway with anything other than water.

» Food heated in the microwave has hot and cold spots. Allow food to "rest" or "stand" for a few minutes; always stir before eating.

Prevent Fires and Electrical Shorts

» Use a power strip or three-pronged outlet—no extension cords or plug adapters.

» In case of fire: leave oven closed. Unplug.

» Monitor microwave while cooking, don't leave unattended.

Quick Eats: Breakfast, Lunch, or Any Time

Whole Wheat Pancakes

Prep Time: 5 min

Cook Time: 10-20 min

Serves: 4

Serving Size: 2 pancakes or 1 slice

INGREDIENTS

1 cup whole wheat flour

2 teaspoon baking powder

¼ teaspoon salt

1 egg

1 cup milk or non dairy alternative

1 tablespoon canola oil or melted butter (optional)

1 cup chopped ripe banana, thin sliced apple, or frozen blueberries (optional)

oil or butter for cooking

DIRECTIONS

Stove Top Directions:

1. Heat a griddle or large skillet over medium-low heat.

2. Mix together dry ingredients in a large bowl; then whisk eggs, milk, and melted butter or oil, if using, in a separate bowl.

3. Gently stir together dry and wet ingredients. Add fruit, if using.

4. Lightly grease pan and spoon ¼ cup batter into hot skillet.

5. Once pancake is bubbling and dry around the edges, flip it.

6. Cook for 3 minutes more or until the center of the pancake is dry. Repeat until batter is finished.

Rice Cooker Directions:

1. Grease a rice cooker with butter or oil.

2. Mix ingredients as described above and pour batter into the rice cooker.

3. Cook covered for 1–2 cycles, or until the cake is dry in the middle.

4. Remove dish from rice cooker and flip it onto a plate. The pancake should pop out.

5. Slice the pancake into four and serve.

Nutrition Facts

Calories	Total Fat	7g	Dietary Fiber	5g
Per serving	Saturated Fat	2g	Sodium	293mg
217	Protein	8g	Carbohydrates	34g

Pumpkin Oatmeal

Prep Time: 20 min

Serves: 3

Serving Size: ⅔ cup

INGREDIENTS

1 cup rolled oats

1½ cups water

½ cup low-fat milk or non-dairy alternative

½ cup canned pumpkin

¼ cup raisins

1 teaspoon cinnamon, nutmeg, or pumpkin pie spice

2 teaspoons honey, maple syrup, or other sweetener (optional)

DIRECTIONS

Stove Top Directions:

1. Heat water over medium heat in a medium pot until bubbles appear.

2. Stir in oats. Cover and lower heat to low.

3. Cook oats until thick, about 5 minutes. Lift lid and stir every minute or two.

4. Stir in milk and other ingredients.

5. Cook for 3-4 more minutes.

Microwave Directions:

1. Mix oats and water in a microwave safe bowl.

2. Cook on high for 2–3 minutes. Stir once during cooking.

3. Add other ingredients, including milk.

4. Heat for 1 more minute or until done. (Timing might be different depending on the microwave.)

Rice Cooker Directions:

1. Put all the ingredients in the rice cooker bowl and cook for one cycle.

Nutrition Facts

Calories	Total Fat		Dietary Fiber	
Per serving	Total Fat	4g	Dietary Fiber	7g
271	Saturated Fat	1g	Sodium	25mg
	Protein	11g	Carbohydrates	50g

One Mug Omelet

Turn leftover bits of meat, vegetables, or herbs into a quick and hearty dish.

Prep Time: 5 min   Serves: 1
Cook Time: 1 min

INGREDIENTS

½ tsp. of olive oil, butter, or cooking spray for greasing

1 large egg

2 tbsp. low-fat milk or water

salt and black pepper, to taste

Optional: your favorite meat, cheese, vegetables, or seasonings

DIRECTIONS

1. Grease a mug with cooking spray, oil, or butter.
2. In a bowl, use a fork to beat the egg, milk or water, salt, and pepper.
3. Chop and mix in your choice of additions.
4. Pour the mixture into the mug.
5. Microwave for 1 minute. Check that egg is fully cooked and not wet. If it's still wet, microwave 30 seconds to 1 minute more.

TIPS

Keep some frozen broccoli or spinach on hand to make this even more quick and easy.

Nutrition Facts

Calories				
Per serving 104	Total Fat	7g	Dietary Fiber	0g
	Saturated Fat	2g	Sodium	85mg
	Protein	7g	Carbohydrates	2g

© Copyright 2018 Leah's Pantry Recipe Booklet

Veggie Egg Scramble

Prep Time: 5 min Serves: 1
Cook Time: 3 min

INGREDIENTS

2 tsp. olive oil

2 eggs

⅓ c. chopped fresh or frozen veggies (spinach, kale, chard, peppers, peas, onion, summer squash, mushrooms)

Optional toppings: cheese, avocado, hot sauce, salsa, etc.

salt and pepper, to taste

DIRECTIONS

1. Sauté veggies in a medium skillet with a teaspoon of olive oil. Place in a medium size bowl.

2. Add 1 teaspoon olive oil to skillet, add eggs, and stir over medium heat.

3. When eggs are partially cooked, add sautéed veggies. Cook until eggs are just set. Add a pinch of salt, pepper, and desired toppings.

TIPS

Serve over some brown rice or in a warmed whole wheat tortilla or pita bread for a complete meal.

Nutrition Facts

Calories	Total Fat	18.5g	Dietary Fiber	<1g
Per serving	Saturated Fat	4g	Sodium	150mg
225	Protein	13g	Carbohydrates	1g

Spring Spread

A tasty dip for veggies or a fun spread on crackers or bagels.

Prep Time: 10 min

Yield: 4

Serving Size: 2 tablespoons

INGREDIENTS

4 ounces low fat cream cheese, whipped or softened (½ package)

½ carrot, coarsely shredded

½ red bell pepper, finely diced

2 green onions, finely chopped

1 tablespoon chopped fresh herbs (such as dill, thyme, oregano, basil) or 1 tsp dried

1 teaspoon freshly squeezed lemon or lime juice

Serve with: sliced veggies, whole grain crackers, toast or bagels

DIRECTIONS

1. Mix all ingredients with a rubber spatula until creamy.

TIPS

Spread on a whole grain flour tortilla, roll up, then slice for mini pinwheel sandwiches.

Nutrition Facts

Calories	Total Fat	4g	Dietary Fiber	<1g
Per serving	Saturated Fat	2.5g	Sodium	106mg
61	Protein	2g	Carbohydrates	3g

Pita Pizza

Prep Time: 10 min
Cook Time: 5-8 min

Serves: 4
Serving Size: 1 mini pizza

INGREDIENTS

4 whole wheat pita bread

1 cup part skim shredded mozzarella cheese

1 cup low-sodium tomato or pizza sauce

1 cup small diced vegetables, such as: bell peppers (green, red, yellow, orange), broccoli, mushrooms, olives, pineapple, onions, tomatoes, asparagus, zucchini, etc.

DIRECTIONS

1. Preheat oven or toaster oven to 425°F. Line baking sheet with foil for easy cleanup.

2. Place the pita on the baking sheet for assembly. Spread the tomato sauce on the pita leaving room for crust.

3. Sprinkle with cheese and add the toppings.

4. Cook pizzas in the oven for 5-8 minutes, or until cheese is melted.

5. Let cool for a minute before eating.

TIPS

Use leftover or frozen veggies to cut down on prep time.

Nutrition Facts

Calories	Total Fat	6g	Dietary Fiber	6g
Per serving	Saturated Fat	3g	Sodium	460mg
213	Protein	13g	Carbohydrates	32g

Hummus and Veggie Wraps

Prep Time: 15 min

Yield: 4

Serving Size: 1 wrap

INGREDIENTS

Hummus:

1 (14.5-oz) can garbanzo beans rinsed and drained (1½ c. cooked)

½ cup plain yogurt or tahini (sesame seed paste)

1 peeled garlic clove

1 tablespoon fresh lemon juice

1 tablespoon ground cumin

salt to taste

Wrap Fixings:

4 whole wheat tortillas, large or burrito size

1 green pepper, sliced

1 large tomato, sliced

2 cups chopped lettuce

DIRECTIONS

1. Puree all hummus ingredients in a blender or food processor until smooth.

2. Refrigerate until ready to use.

3. Spread hummus on tortilla. Layer veggies. Roll up and eat!

TIPS

No blender? No problem! Just use the back of a fork or potato masher to mash up the garbanzo beans and grate/finely mince the garlic before stirring in the remaining ingredients.

Nutrition Facts

Calories	Total Fat	6g	Dietary Fiber	9g
Per serving 221	Saturated Fat	2g	Sodium	464mg
	Protein	11g	Carbohydrates	34g

Southwest Baked Potatoes

Prep Time: 30 min   Yield: 2

Serving Size: 1 potato

INGREDIENTS

2 medium-sized sweet potatoes
or large russet potatoes

1 (15-oz.) can low-sodium black
beans, rinsed

1 medium tomato, diced

2 teaspoons olive oil

½ teaspoon ground cumin

½ teaspoon chili powder

¼ teaspoon salt

sour cream, chopped scallions,
chopped cilantro (optional)

DIRECTIONS

1. Pierce potatoes in several places with a fork.

2. Bake for 40-50 minutes in a 350° F oven or microwave potatoes on high 12-15 minutes, until tender.

3. Combine beans, tomatoes, oil, cumin, chili powder, and salt. Heat in the microwave (2-3 minutes) or on the stove.

4. Slice each potato down the middle. Press open, making a well in the center.

5. Spoon the bean mixture into middle of each potato.

6. If desired, top with sour cream, scallions, or cilantro.

Nutrition Facts

Calories	Total Fat	4g	Dietary Fiber	14g
Per serving	Saturated Fat	<1g	Sodium	427mg
311	Protein	14g	Carbohydrates	57g

Tasty Tostada

Using pre-cooked chicken makes this a no-cook meal.

Prep Time: 15 min

Serves: 4

Serving Size: 1 tostada

INGREDIENTS

2 cups shredded romaine lettuce or cabbage

4 pieces tostada shells or crispy taco shells

2 cups cooked ground or chopped chicken

1 cup prepared salsa (try the Salsa Fresca recipe on page 51)

½ cup canned corn

½ cup low sodium canned black beans

¼ cup shredded cheddar or Jack cheese

DIRECTIONS

1. Place ½ cup shredded lettuce or cabbage on each tostada shell.

2. Put chicken and salsa in a small bowl and stir.

3. Spoon about ½ cup chicken mixture onto each tostada.

4. Top each tostada with 2 tablespoons corn, 2 tablespoons black beans, and 1 tablespoon cheese before serving.

Nutrition Facts

Calories	Total Fat	7g	Dietary Fiber	5g
Per serving 271	Saturated Fat	2g	Sodium	351mg
	Protein	28g	Carbohydrates	25g

Vegetable Noodle Bowl

Prep/Cook: 20 min

Optional Chilling: 60 min

Serves: 8

Serving Size: 2 cups

INGREDIENTS

- 1 pound whole wheat spaghetti
- 3 tablespoons low-sodium soy sauce
- 4 teaspoons toasted sesame oil
- 1 teaspoon hot chili sauce (like Siracha), or to taste
- 2 garlic cloves, finely minced or grated
- 1 bunch scallions, chopped (about 1 cup)

- 1 cucumber, cut in half lengthwise and thinly sliced (about 1 cup)
- 2 carrots, coarsely grated (about 1 cup)
- ¼-½ head of cabbage, shredded (about 1 cup)

- salt and pepper, to taste
- 1 cup diced firm tofu (optional)

DIRECTIONS

1. Prepare the noodles according to the package instructions. Rinse them under cold water and put them in a colander to drain.

2. In a large bowl, mix the soy sauce, sesame oil, chili sauce, scallions, garlic, cucumber, carrot, and cabbage. Add the noodles toss everything together with a fork or a tongs. Gently stir in tofu, if using. Taste it and add salt and pepper as needed.

3. Let the noodles sit in the fridge for about an hour if you can. The flavors will mingle and become more intense.

Nutrition Facts

Calories	Total Fat	4g	Dietary Fiber	6g
Per serving	Saturated Fat	<1g	Sodium	238mg
237	Protein	9g	Carbohydrates	45g

Souped-Up Soup

This recipe is a way to make a common pantry item more nutritious.

Prep Time: 8-10 min
Cook Time: 5-8 min

Serves: 2
Serving Size: 1 cup

INGREDIENTS

1 (14.5-oz) can low-sodium condensed soup

½ onion, chopped

1 stalk celery, chopped

1 potato, cut in small cubes

1 carrot, diced

black pepper or chili pepper, to taste

DIRECTIONS

Stove Top Directions:

1. Pour one can of condensed soup into a skillet with one can of water.
2. Add chopped vegetables.
3. Cook soup on medium until vegetables are tender.
4. Season to taste.

Rice Cooker Directions:

1. Put all ingredients in the cooker.
2. Set the "cook" for one cycle, or until vegetables are soft.

Microwave Directions:

1. Put all ingredients in a microwave-safe bowl.
2. Heat on medium-high for 4–5 or until vegetables are soft. Stir once or twice during cooking.

TIPS

Use dried spices such as chili or garlic powder to add flavor without salt.

Nutrition Facts *(can vary depending on the type of soup used)*

Calories	Total Fat	1g	Dietary Fiber	7g
Per serving 205	Saturated Fat	<1g	Sodium	218mg
	Protein	6g	Carbohydrates	45g

Making Boxed Meals Healthier

General Tips:

» If most of your meals come from a box, add roasted or sautéed vegetables to boost the nutrition.

» Using half of the seasoning packet decreases the amount of sodium and other additives. Add your own seasonings for more flavor.

Ramen Noodles and Cup o' Noodles

Cook noodles as directed, but add half of flavoring package. Add cubes of cooked chicken and either your favorite frozen vegetable medley or partially cooked fresh vegetables. Adding meat and vegetables stretches the dish to four servings.

Macaroni and Cheese

Cook the box of macaroni and cheese as directed. Add defrosted vegetables such as spinach or broccoli, or cook cauliflower, onions, or other vegetables in the microwave until soft.

Make Your Own Snack Box

Prepackaged lunch boxes of crackers, sliced cheese, and dessert are low in nutritional value, not to mention expensive. Portion out your own from whole grain crackers, cheese you slice yourself, carrot sticks, and apple slices.

Avocado, Rice, and Beans

This can be a quick meal or snack if you keep cooked rice on hand.

Prep Time: 10 min   Serves: 2

Cook Time: 45 min   Serving Size: 2 cups

INGREDIENTS

½ cup uncooked brown rice

1 (15-oz.) can low-sodium beans (kidney, pinto, black, or other kind)

1 avocado

Optional spices: black pepper, garlic powder, ground cumin

DIRECTIONS

1. Bring 1 cup of water to a boil with ½ tsp. salt (optional). Stir in rice. Cover and cook over low heat until water is absorbed, about 45 minutes, or cook rice in a rice cooker.

2. Meanwhile, rinse and drain beans. Add desired spices. Cook over low heat in a small saucepan, or in the microwave.

3. Cut avocado into slices or dice into small pieces. Serve rice with beans on top, and garnish with avocado pieces.

TIPS

This dish can be topped with a variety of add-ons. Try hot sauce, salsa, sautéed greens, or a fried egg.

Nutrition Facts

Calories	Total Fat	17g	Dietary Fiber	18g
Per serving	Saturated Fat	3g	Sodium	222mg
511	Protein	17g	Carbohydrates	76g

Stews, Stir Fries, and One Pot Meals

Easy Meatballs and Sauce

Prep Time: 20 min

Cook Time: 18-22 min or 6-8 hr

Serves: 4

Serving Size: 3 meatballs

INGREDIENTS

1 pound lean ground meat (turkey, chicken, or beef)

1 cup bread crumbs

2 teaspoons Italian seasoning (or dried oregano or basil)

3 cloves of garlic, finely minced

1 small onion, finely diced or coarsely grated

2 eggs, beaten

salt and pepper, to taste

1 (28-oz.) can low-sodium crushed tomatoes

DIRECTIONS

Stove Top Directions:

1. Mix first seven ingredients (everything except tomatoes) in a bowl until combined. Form into 12 meatballs.

2. Pour tomatoes into pot. Bring to a simmer. Lower heat.

3. Gently add meatballs into the mixture.

4. Cook for 18-22 minutes until cooked through.

Slow Cooker Directions:

1. Prepare meatballs as in step 1 above. Pour tomatoes into a 2-4 quart slow cooker. Add meatballs.

2. Cook on LOW for 6 to 8 hours.

TIPS

Serve with whole wheat pasta or crusty Italian bread. Leftover meatballs store well in the freezer.

Nutrition Facts

Calories				
Per serving	Total Fat	15g	Dietary Fiber	7g
452	Saturated Fat	4g	Sodium	477mg
	Protein	36g	Carbohydrates	46g

Vegetable Stew with Coconut Milk

Prep Time: 10 min   Serves: 6

Cook Time: 30 min   Serving Size: 1 cup

INGREDIENTS

1 teaspoon vegetable oil

1 small onion, diced

2 garlic cloves, minced

1 small butternut squash or 2 sweet potatoes, peeled and diced into 2-inch chunks

1 small bunch collard greens or kale, cut into bite sized pieces

1 (14-oz.) can coconut milk

2 cups water

1 tablespoon soy sauce

chili flakes, to taste

1 pound fish fillets, shrimp, or boneless, skinless chicken OR 1 can (15-oz) garbanzo beans (optional)

juice of 1 lime

DIRECTIONS

1. In a large pot, heat oil and sauté onion and garlic for 2 minutes.

2. Add the squash, greens, coconut milk, water, soy sauce, and chili flakes. Simmer for 20 minutes, stirring occasionally.

3. In the meantime, prepare choice of protein with a pinch of salt, if using. Cut the fish into large chunks or the chicken into bite sized pieces. Leave shrimp whole. Drain the garbanzo beans.

4. When the vegetables are tender, add protein to the pot. Cover and cook about 7-10 more minutes, or until meat is cooked through.

5. Squeeze lime juice over everything before serving.

TIPS

Serve with cooked rice, quinoa, or another grain. Top this dish with chopped cilantro, basil or green onions for even more color and flavor!

Nutrition Facts

Calories	Total Fat	17g	Dietary Fiber	6g
Per serving 254	Saturated Fat	13g	Sodium	389mg
	Protein	7g	Carbohydrates	24g

Ralph's Mediterranean Beef Stew

This recipe was a signature dish of a beloved Leah's Pantry staff member, Ralph Cooper, the slow-cooker chef.

Prep Time: 10 min

Cook Time: 5-7 hours

Serves: 4

Serving Size: 2 cups

INGREDIENTS

- 1 potato, cut into 1-inch pieces (about 1 cup)
- 1 carrot, cut into 1-inch pieces (about 1 cup)
- 1 large zucchini, chopped (about 2 cups)
- 1 pound beef stew meat, fat trimmed and cut into ½-inch pieces

- 1 (14½-oz.) can of Italian-style diced tomatoes
- ¼ teaspoon ground black pepper
- ¼ teaspoon cinnamon
- 1 teaspoon salt

DIRECTIONS

1. Place potatoes, carrots and zucchini in the bottom of a 2-4 quart slow cooker.
2. Add beef and remaining ingredients.
3. Cover and cook on HIGH for 5 hours or until meat is tender. Or, cover and cook on HIGH 1 hour, then reduce to LOW heat and cook on LOW for 7 hours.

TIPS

Substitute some or all of the potatoes with other root vegetables such as turnips, rutabaga, celery, or parsnips.

Nutrition Facts

Calories	Total Fat	8g	Dietary Fiber	5g
Per serving 296	Saturated Fat	<1g	Sodium	556mg
	Protein	40g	Carbohydrates	17g

40

© Copyright 2018 Leah's Pantry Recipe Booklet

Secret Ingredient Veggie Chili

Cocoa powder gives a rich flavor to this dish.

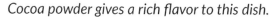

Prep Time: 10-12 min

Cook Time: 35 min or 4-8 hr

Serves: 7

Serving Size: 2 cups

INGREDIENTS

1 tablespoon olive or canola oil

1 large onion, chopped

1 green bell pepper, chopped

2 cups chopped butternut squash or sweet potato

4 garlic cloves chopped

2 teaspoons chili powder

2 teaspoons ground cumin

2 teaspoons unsweetened cocoa powder

2 (14-oz.) cans low-sodium diced tomatoes, preferably fire-roasted

4 (15-oz.) cans low-sodium cooked beans (approximately 4 cups)

1 cup water

½ teaspoon salt

½ teaspoon pepper

DIRECTIONS

Stove Top Directions:

1. In a large pot, heat oil and sauté onion and bell pepper until soft. Add sweet potato, garlic, chili powder, and cumin, then sauté two more minutes.

2. Add remaining ingredients. Bring to a boil, then reduce heat and simmer for 30 minutes. Stir during cooking to prevent sticking.

Slow Cooker Directions:

1. Combine all ingredients except oil in the slow cooker and cook on LOW for 7-8 hours, or HIGH for 4 hours, or until the chili has thickened and the vegetables are cooked.

Nutrition Facts

Calories	Total Fat	4g	Dietary Fiber	14g
Per serving	Saturated Fat	<1g	Sodium	367mg
289	Protein	15g	Carbohydrates	50g

Tuna Pasta Marinara

Prep Time: 5 min

Cook Time: 10 min

Serves: 4

Serving Size: 2 cups

INGREDIENTS

1½ cups low sodium spaghetti sauce

1 small (5-oz.) can tuna packed in oil or water, drained

2 tablespoons diced olives

1 tablespoon dried basil or oregano

black pepper, to taste

2 tablespoons chopped fresh parsley, optional

zest of 1 lemon, optional

½ pound whole wheat pasta

DIRECTIONS

1. Prepare pasta according to package directions.

2. In the meantime, combine the sauce, tuna, olives, dried basil or oregano in a small pot, rice cooker, or microwave.

3. Cook to blend the flavors. Break up tuna, if necessary. This takes about 5 minutes in the pot or 1 cycle of the rice cooker. If using the microwave, cover and heat for 2 minutes; stir, cover, and heat for another minute.

4. Season with pepper and lemon zest. Toss sauce with pasta and additional seasonings.

TIPS

If you don't have a zester, use a vegetable peeler to remove strip of lemon peel (just the yellow part!) then finely chop.

Nutrition Facts

Calories	Total Fat	4g	Dietary Fiber	4g
Per serving 312	Saturated Fat	<1g	Sodium	198mg
	Protein	17g	Carbohydrates	51g

Pineapple Chicken Stir Fry

Prep Time: 10 min   Serves: 4

Cook Time: 15 min   Serving Size: 2 cups

INGREDIENTS

1 tablespoon canola oil

1 pound boneless skinless chicken, cut into 1-in. cubes

1 red bell pepper, cut into the same size as the chicken

1 small onion, cut into the same size as the chicken

1 cup canned pineapple chunks, plus ¼ cup juice

¼ teaspoon red pepper flakes, more if desired

2 tablespoons ketchup

2 tablespoons soy sauce

1 teaspoon garlic powder

½ teaspoon ground ginger

black pepper, to taste

2 cups cooked brown rice

DIRECTIONS

1. In a small bowl, stir together ¼ cup pineapple juice, pepper flakes, ketchup, soy sauce, garlic and ginger, to make sauce.

2. Heat a large skillet with oil. Sauté chicken over medium high heat until cooked through, about 8 minutes.

3. Add bell pepper and onion to the skillet and sauté for 3 minutes.

4. Add sauce. Cook and stir for about 2 minutes until vegetables are cooked through but still bright and crunchy, and sauce is thick.

5. Add 1 cup pineapple to wok or skillet and cook until hot. Season with black pepper to taste.

6. Serve stir-fry over ½ cup of brown rice.

TIPS

Make sure to use pineapple packed in juice, not syrup. You can also substitute canned mandarin oranges in juice to make orange chicken.

Nutrition Facts

Calories	Total Fat	9g	Dietary Fiber	4g
Per serving	Saturated Fat	2g	Sodium	662mg
478	Protein	41g	Carbohydrates	56g

Fried Rice

Total Time: 30 min   Serves: 4

Serving Size: 1 cup

INGREDIENTS

3 teaspoons vegetable oil

1 cup firm tofu, shrimp, or chopped meat, optional

1 clove garlic minced

2 cups diced raw vegetables

1 egg beaten

2 cups cooked rice, cold

2 tablespoons soy sauce

black pepper, to taste

DIRECTIONS

1. Heat 1 teaspoon oil until sizzling in the bottom of skillet.

2. Add tofu, shrimp or meat to the skillet, if using, and cook through. Remove from pan and set aside.

3. Return pan to the stove. Add and heat remaining 2 teaspoons oil.

4. Add garlic and vegetables. Stir fry vegetables until slightly brown and tender.

5. Add the egg directly into the base of the pan. Allow it to scramble by stirring it back and forth across the hot pan.

6. Add rice, soy sauce, black pepper and meat. Turn heat down to medium low. Cook until heated through, stirring frequently.

TIPS

Try this with: onion, celery, bell pepper, asparagus, cabbage, broccoli, green beans, peas, zucchini, mushrooms, or bean sprouts.

Nutrition Facts

Calories	Total Fat	5g	Dietary Fiber	4g
Per serving 242	Saturated Fat	<1g	Sodium	561mg
	Protein	7g	Carbohydrates	42g

Chicken, Rice, and Vegetables

Improvise on this dish with your own favorite seasonings and vegetables. Try making it with Indian, Cajun, Mexican, or Italian seasonings.

Prep Time: 15 min	Serves: 4
Cook Time: 30 min	Serving Size: 1 cup

INGREDIENTS

8 oz. raw boneless and skinless chicken or cooked chicken sausage, cut into ½ inch pieces (about 2 cups)

2 ½ cups low-sodium chicken broth and/or water

1 cup brown rice (or other grain)

1 cup assorted vegetables chopped into bite-sized pieces

dried herbs or seasoning of your choice

salt and pepper, to taste

DIRECTIONS

Stove Top Directions:

1. Layer items into a 2 quart pot in the order that they are listed (starting with meat on bottom).

2. Cover and cook on low heat for 30 minutes until broth is absorbed and chicken is cooked through.

Rice Cooker Directions:

1. Layer ingredients in rice cooker.

2. Cover and cook for a normal cycle.

TIPS

A can of drained and rinsed beans can also be added to the pot for extra fiber.

Nutrition Facts

Calories	Total Fat	4g	Dietary Fiber	3g
Per serving	Saturated Fat	1g	Sodium	114mg
291	Protein	23g	Carbohydrates	39g

Quinoa, Chickpeas, and Greens

Prep Time: 5 min

Cook Time: 20 min

Serves: 4

Serving Size: 1 cup

INGREDIENTS

1 cup quinoa, rinsed

2 cups water

3 cups greens (mustard, kale, collard greens), chopped

1 cup canned chickpeas

⅓ cup dried cranberries

3 tablespoons olive oil

6 tablespoons lemon juice

salt and pepper, to taste

DIRECTIONS

Stove Top Directions:

1. Put everything in a pot and cover.

2. Cook over medium heat. Stir twice while cooking.

Rice Cooker Directions:

1. Mix all ingredients in rice cooker and cook for a normal cycle. Stir twice while cooking.

TIPS

Rinse the quinoa before cooking for better flavor.

Nutrition Facts

Calories	Total Fat	14g	Dietary Fiber	8g
Per serving 352	Saturated Fat	2g	Sodium	192mg
	Protein	10g	Carbohydrates	49g

Soups, Sides, and Salads

Sweet Potato Apple Soup

Double this recipe to make it for a crowd or to freeze some for later.

Prep Time: 15 min   Serves: 4

Cook Time: 25 min   Serving Size: 1 cups

INGREDIENTS

1 tablespoon butter, coconut oil, or olive oil

1 small onion, chopped

1 garlic clove, minced

1 Granny Smith apple, washed, cored, and chopped (don't peel)

1 large sweet potato, washed and cut into ½-inch pieces (don't peel)

¼ teaspoon ginger powder

¼ teaspoon black pepper

⅛ teaspoon cayenne pepper (optional)

1½ cups vegetable broth

1½ cups water

salt, to taste

DIRECTIONS

1. Heat oil or melt butter in a large stockpot over medium heat. Add onion and garlic and cook until golden.

2. Add apples, sweet potatoes, cayenne pepper, black pepper, broth, and water. Bring to a boil.

3. Reduce heat to low and simmer until the sweet potatoes are soft, about 25 minutes.

4. Add salt to taste and adjust the seasonings.

5. Use a blender to puree until smooth. Be careful when blending hot liquids. Blend small amounts at a time and start on slowest settings.

TIPS

If you don't have a blender, just peel the apples and sweet potatoes before cooking. Then mash everything up with a masher or large spoon after its done.

Nutrition Facts

Calories	Total Fat	4g	Dietary Fiber	4g
Per serving 153	Saturated Fat	<1g	Sodium	128mg
	Protein	4g	Carbohydrates	26g

Turkey Rice Soup with Ginger

Prep Time: 15 min   Serves: 6

Cook Time: 40 min or 3½-7 hr   Serving Size: 2 cups

INGREDIENTS

4 cups low sodium broth or water

1 pound raw boneless, skinless turkey or chicken, cut into 1-inch pieces

8 oz. mushrooms, sliced

1 cup water

2 carrots, thinly sliced

1 medium onion, finely chopped

2 tablespoons soy sauce

2 teaspoons grated fresh ginger

4 cloves garlic, minced

1 cup brown rice

1½ cup greens (such as bok choy, watercress, or spinach)

DIRECTIONS

Stove top or rice cooker directions:

1. Place all ingredients besides greens into the pot or rice cooker.
2. Cover and simmer for 40 minutes.
3. Add greens, cover for 5 more minutes or until greens have wilted.

Slow cooker directions:

1. Place all ingredients besides greens into the slow cooker.
2. Cover and cook on low for 7 hours or on HIGH for 3½ hours.
3. Add greens, cover for 5-10 more minutes or until greens have wilted.

TIPS

If you have some leftover cooked chicken or turkey on hand, substitute about 3 cups chopped meat for the raw meat.

Nutrition Facts

Calories	Total Fat	5g	Dietary Fiber	3g
Per serving 248	Saturated Fat	1g	Sodium	480mg
	Protein	18g	Carbohydrates	33g

Hearty Vegetable Soup

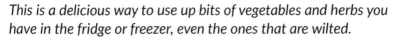

This is a delicious way to use up bits of vegetables and herbs you have in the fridge or freezer, even the ones that are wilted.

Prep Time: 10 min

Cook Time: 25-30 min

Serves: 4

Serving Size: 2 cups

INGREDIENTS

3 tablespoons olive oil

1 large onion, diced

1 teaspoon cumin

2 cloves garlic, finely chopped

2 medium potatoes, diced

3 tomatoes, chopped (or a 14.5-oz can chopped tomatoes)

4 cups chopped vegetables: carrot, zucchini or yellow squash, bell pepper, celery, asparagus, corn, peas, okra, green beans, spinach, kale, mushrooms, cabbage, or lima beans

4 cups vegetable broth

2 cups water

juice from ½ lemon, more if desired

salt and pepper, to taste

DIRECTIONS

1. In a stock pot, sauté the onion and celery (if using) in the olive oil until golden. Add garlic and cumin and cook a minute longer.

2. Add the potatoes (and any root vegetables, such as carrots), tomatoes, broth, water, and oregano. Bring to a boil and simmer until the potatoes are tender.

3. Add the other vegetables and simmer until everything is soft.

4. Stir in lemon juice. Season with salt and pepper, to taste.

TIPS

Try at least three different kinds of vegetables in this recipe.

Nutrition Facts

Calories	Total Fat	7g	Dietary Fiber	5g
Per serving 156	Saturated Fat	1g	Sodium	522mg
	Protein	4g	Carbohydrates	21g

Salsa Fresca

This salsa can be enjoyed with chips, burritos, or tacos, as well as a topping for eggs, meat, or fish.

Prep Time: 15 min

Serves: 4

Serving Size: ½ cup

INGREDIENTS

3 sprigs fresh cilantro (stems included)

1 small red onion

1 medium green bell pepper

hot sauce or fresh hot peppers, to taste (optional)

6 plum tomatoes

2 tablespoons red wine vinegar

1 lime, juiced

1 tablespoon ground cumin

1 teaspoon olive oil

salt, to taste

DIRECTIONS

1. Roughly chop the cilantro. Cut the onion and peppers into large pieces. Process in a blender until coarsely chopped.

2. Quarter the tomatoes. Add, along with remaining ingredients and pulse until the mixture is chopped into small pieces.

3. Serve immediately, or cover and chill for up to three days.

TIPS

Prepare this without a blender by chopping everything finely with a knife and grating the tomatoes on the large holes of a grater (over a bowl so you catch the juices!).

Nutrition Facts

Calories	Total Fat	2g	Dietary Fiber	3g
Per serving	Saturated Fat	<1g	Sodium	12mg
58	Protein	2g	Carbohydrates	10g

Garlicky Roasted Vegetables

Roasting brings out the natural sweetness of many vegetables.

Prep Time: 20 min   Serves: 2

Cook Time: 10-20 min   Serving Size: 1 cup

INGREDIENTS

2 tablespoons olive oil

salt and pepper, to taste

Other spices, to taste (optional)

2 cups non-leafy vegetables such as potatoes, squash, beets, carrots, cauliflower, or broccoli, chopped

2 cloves garlic, minced

DIRECTIONS

1. Preheat oven to about 450° F.

2. Place vegetables in a bowl. Toss to coat with olive oil and spices.

3. Spread vegetables in a layer on a baking pan.

4. Place on middle rack and cook vegetables for about 10 minutes.

5. Carefully remove pan from oven, sprinkle garlic, and flip them.

6. Cook vegetables until tender and nicely browned, 10-20 minutes more.

Nutrition Facts

Calories	Total Fat	14g	Dietary Fiber	6g
Per serving	Saturated Fat	2g	Sodium	57mg
206	Protein	4g	Carbohydrates	18g

52

Sautéed Vegetables

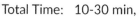

Total Time: 10-30 min, depending on vegetables chosen

Serves: 3

INGREDIENTS

2 tablespoons olive oil or canola oil

1 clove garlic, minced

1 pound vegetables

dried seasonings of your choice

salt and black pepper, to taste

DIRECTIONS

1. Wash and/or peel the veggies as needed and cut into ½-inch pieces or slices.

2. In a medium sauté pan, heat oil with garlic. Add the vegetables and cook for about one minute. If using a variety of vegetables, add the firmer vegetables to the pan first and cook for a few minutes before adding the faster cooking vegetables.

3. Add the dried seasonings. Cover and cook for 3-5 more minutes, or until the vegetables are tender.

4. Sprinkle with salt and pepper and seasonings to taste.

TIPS

Letting the vegetable brown slightly makes them extra flavorful.

Nutrition Facts

Calories	Total Fat	10g	Dietary Fiber	5g
Per serving	Saturated Fat	1g	Sodium	249mg
123	Protein	5g	Carbohydrates	7g

Corn, Blueberry, and Wild Rice Salad

Prep Time: 15 min

Chill Time: 1 hr (optional)

Serves: 6

Serving Size: 1 cup

INGREDIENTS

2 tablespoons lemon juice, about ½ lemon

2 tablespoons olive oil

2 teaspoons honey

½ teaspoon ground cumin

½ teaspoon salt

1½ cups fresh or frozen corn kernels

1 cup fresh or frozen blueberries

1 cup cooked wild rice or brown rice, slightly warm

1 cucumber, finely diced

¼ cup finely diced red onion or sliced scallions

¼ cup chopped fresh cilantro

DIRECTIONS

1. Make the dressing: In a large serving bowl combine lemon juice, olive oil, honey, cumin, and salt. Whisk together with a fork.

2. Add corn, blueberries, rice, cucumber, red onion, and cilantro. Stir together all ingredients to coat them evenly with dressing.

3. Serve immediately, or cover and refrigerate 1 hour to let flavors meld.

TIPS

The rice will absorb flavors better if mixed with the dressing while a little warm. If using leftover cold rice, microwave or steam it briefly to reheat.

If you need to make rice: Bring 1 cup rice, water (2¼ cups for brown, 3 cups for wild), and a pinch of salt to a boil. Reduce heat to low and simmer, covered, until the rice is tender and most of the liquid has been absorbed, 40 to 50 minutes. Let stand 5 minutes, then fluff with a fork. This basic recipe will make 3 cups of cooked rice, so save some for another time.

Nutrition Facts

Calories	Total Fat	5g	Dietary Fiber	3g
Per serving 157	Saturated Fat	<1g	Sodium	226mg
	Protein	4g	Carbohydrates	27g

Black Bean and Corn Salad

This also makes a great taco filling or topping for tortilla chips.

Prep Time: 20 min

Serves: 6

Serving Size: 1 cup

INGREDIENTS

1 (15-oz.) can black beans, rinsed and drained

1 (15-oz.) cans whole kernel corn, drained or 2 cups corn kernels (fresh or frozen, defrosted)

4 green onions, chopped

1 green bell pepper, chopped

2 small tomatoes seeded and chopped

1 jalapeño pepper, seeded and minced (optional)

1 avocado peeled, pitted and diced (optional)

1 lime, juiced

¼ teaspoon garlic powder

½ teaspoon chili powder

½ teaspoon cumin ground

2 tablespoons olive oil

DIRECTIONS

» Combine ingredients in a large bowl. Chill for an hour, if possible, before serving.

TIPS

Some jalapeños can be mild while others are spicy. Taste a tiny piece before deciding how much you want to add.

Nutrition Facts

Calories	Total Fat	10g	Dietary Fiber	10g
Per serving	Saturated Fat	1.5g	Sodium	440mg
228	Protein	8g	Carbohydrates	31g

Pear, Grape, and Cucumber Salad

Prep Time: 20 min

Serves: 4

Serving Size: 1 cup

INGREDIENTS

2 teaspoons olive oil

2 tablespoons fresh lime juice

⅛ teaspoon salt or to taste

1 large cucumber, diced (peel if waxed)

1½ cups seedless red grapes, sliced in half

2 pears, diced

DIRECTIONS

1. In a large bowl, whisk oil, lime juice, and salt.
2. Add grapes, cucumber, and pears and toss.

TIPS

Sprinkle with ground chile for a little kick.

Nutrition Facts

Calories	Total Fat	2g	Dietary Fiber	2g
Per serving 73	Saturated Fat	<1g	Sodium	52mg
	Protein	<1g	Carbohydrates	16g

Fruity Spinach Salad

This recipe uses Fuyu Persimmons which are only available in the wintertime. Try mandarin oranges, strawberries, or peaches, if persimmons are not available.

Prep Time: 15 min

Serves: 4

Serving Size: 2 cups

INGREDIENTS

Dressing:

1½ tablespoons olive oil

3 tablespoons orange juice

2 tablespoons unseasoned rice vinegar (no added salt or sugar)

½ teaspoon salt

Salad:

5 cups packed fresh baby spinach, washed

3 medium Fuyu persimmons, sliced

½ cup dried cranberries

½ cup toasted pecans, walnuts, or almonds, coarsely chopped (optional)

DIRECTIONS

1. In a jar with a tight fitting lid, combine oil, orange juice, rice vinegar and salt for the dressing. Shake well. Or everything together in a small bowl.

2. In a large bowl, combine spinach, persimmons, cranberries, and nuts. Toss salad with dressing and serve.

Nutrition Facts

Calories	Total Fat	5g	Dietary Fiber	1g
Per serving	Saturated Fat	<1g	Sodium	160mg
90	Protein	1g	Carbohydrates	11g

Apple Celery Slaw

Prep Time: 20 min

Serves: 6

Serving Size: 1 cup

INGREDIENTS

1 tablespoon apple cider vinegar

¼ teaspoon Dijon or brown mustard

2 tablespoons olive oil

3 apples diced (skin on)

2 large celery ribs cut into ¼ inch-thick pieces

2 cups shredded raw cabbage

¼ cup roasted nuts, chopped

DIRECTIONS

1. Whisk the vinegar with the mustard in a large bowl.
2. Add oil in a stream, whisking until blended.
3. Toss apples, celery, and cabbage with dressing.
4. Just before serving, sprinkle with nuts.

TIPS

For vibrant color, try red cabbage with green apples or green cabbage with red apples.

Nutrition Facts

Calories	Total Fat	8g	Dietary Fiber	3g
Per serving 123	Saturated Fat	1g	Sodium	24mg
	Protein	2g	Carbohydrates	13g

Treats

Green Smoothie

Prep Time: 5 min   Serves: 1

INGREDIENTS

1 large handful raw greens such as spinach or kale (about 1 cup)

½ medium banana

1 cup other chopped fresh or frozen fruit

1 cup low fat milk or milk substitute

DIRECTIONS

1. Place all ingredients in a blender in the order listed.

2. Blend until smooth and creamy. Add a little water if desired for a thinner smoothie.

TIPS

Use frozen fruit for a thicker, colder smoothie

Nutrition Facts

Calories	Total Fat	1.5g	Dietary Fiber	6g
Per serving	Saturated Fat	<1g	Sodium	129mg
218	Protein	10g	Carbohydrates	45g

Popcorn with Toppings

Popcorn can be a healthy, high fiber snack, especially if you pop your own.

Prep Time: 10 min

Serves: 5

Serving Size: 3 cups

INGREDIENTS

½ cup popcorn kernels

2 tablespoons oil

Assorted toppings such as soy sauce, balsamic vinegar, garlic powder, lemon pepper, cinnamon, paprika, cayenne pepper, red pepper flakes, nutritional yeast

DIRECTIONS

1. Add oil to a large pot with a lid.

2. Add popcorn kernels, cover, and heat on medium. You will hear the kernels begin to pop after a few minutes.

3. Shake the pan frequently, holding the lid in place, to make sure all the kernels cook evenly without burning.

4. When you hear the popping slow down, remove from heat. Carefully open the lid.

Nutrition Facts

Calories	Total Fat	6g	Dietary Fiber	3g
Per serving	Saturated Fat	<1g	Sodium	<1mg*
135	Protein	3g	Carbohydrates	18g

*without toppings

Yogurt Parfaits

Carefully read the labels on the yogurt, granola, and cereal you buy.
Many have a lot of added sugar.

Prep Time: 15

Serves: 4

Serving Size: 1½ cup

INGREDIENTS

2 cups fresh or frozen fruit, at least two different kinds

2 cup plain unsweetened yogurt

2 tablespoons 100% fruit spread or honey

1 cup low sugar granola or dry cereal

DIRECTIONS

1. Wash and cut fruit into small pieces.

2. In a bowl, mix the yogurt and fruit spread together.

3. Layer each of the four parfaits as follows: ¼ cup fruit, ¼ cup yogurt, 2 tablespoons granola (repeat).

TIPS

Combine all ingredients except the granola the night before for a quick breakfast.

Nutrition Facts

Calories	Total Fat	7g	Dietary Fiber	4g
Per serving 272	Saturated Fat	4g	Sodium	137mg
	Protein	9g	Carbohydrates	44g

Banana Sushi

As fast and delicious as a PB&J, but much more fun to make.

Prep Time: 5 min

Serves: 2

Serving Size: ½ roll or 4 pieces

INGREDIENTS

1 8-inch soft whole wheat tortilla

2 tablespoons all natural peanut butter

cinnamon, to taste

1 banana, peeled

1 tablespoon raisins

DIRECTIONS

1. Spread a layer of peanut butter across the tortilla. Leave a gap at the edge about as wide as your fingertip.
2. Sprinkle with raisins.
3. Shake cinnamon on top of the peanut butter.
4. Place the peeled banana in the middle of the tortilla.
5. Roll the tortilla tightly.
6. Cut into 8 pieces.

TIPS

Try to find peanut butter with nothing in it but peanuts and salt. Avoid peanut butters with added oil or sugar.

Nutrition Facts

Calories	Total Fat	11g	Dietary Fiber	5g
Per serving	Saturated Fat	3g	Sodium	185mg
232	Protein	7g	Carbohydrates	31g

Banana Oat Muffins

Prep Time: 10 min
Cook Time: 15-18 min

Serves: 12
Serving Size: 1 muffin

INGREDIENTS

2 tablespoons melted butter, coconut oil or canola oil

½ cup brown sugar

2 eggs

1 cup packed mashed ripe bananas (about 2-3 bananas)

½ cup milk

1 teaspoon baking soda

1 teaspoon vanilla extract

½ teaspoon salt

½ teaspoon cinnamon

1½ cups whole wheat flour

½ cup oats

½ cup chopped walnuts or pecans (optional)

DIRECTIONS

1. Preheat the oven to 375° F. Line muffin tin with paper liners or grease with butter or non-stick cooking spray.

2. In a large bowl, whisk together the oil and brown sugar. Add the eggs and beat well. Mix in the mashed bananas and milk, followed by the baking soda, vanilla extract, salt, and cinnamon.

3. Add the flour, oats, and nuts to the bowl and mix just until combined.

4. Divide the batter evenly between the muffin cups, filling each cup about two-thirds full. Bake muffins for 15-18 minutes, or until a toothpick inserted into a muffin comes out clean.

5. Cool slightly before removing from the pan.

TIPS

Pureed sweet potatoes, apple sauce, or canned pumpkin can be used instead of the banana.

Nutrition Facts

Calories	Total Fat	4g	Dietary Fiber	5g
Per serving 164	Saturated Fat	<1g	Sodium	166mg
	Protein	5g	Carbohydrates	29g

Cocoa Rice

This chocolaty rice pudding can be eaten for breakfast, snack, or dessert.

Prep Time: 5 min   Serves: 4
Cook Time: 45-60 min   Serving Size: 1 cup

INGREDIENTS

1 cup brown or white rice

4 cups water

¼ cup ground unsweetened cacao or cocoa powder

¼ cup coconut milk

1 tablespoon honey, maple syrup, or brown sugar

DIRECTIONS

1. Rinse rice. Combine with water in a medium saucepan. Bring to a boil, cover and reduce heat. Simmer for about 40 minutes, stirring occasionally. (Brown rice may need 10-15 minutes more to soften completely.)

2. When rice is soft, add cocoa powder, coconut milk and sweetener. Whisk to combine, then cover and simmer gently for 5 minutes. If needed, stir in a bit of water to thin.

3. Serve warm, or transfer to small bowls and chill.

TIPS

Add 1 or 2 wide ribbons of orange peel to the rice as it cooks to infuse it with a hint of fruitiness.

Nutrition Facts

Calories	Total Fat	5g	Dietary Fiber	4g
Per serving	Saturated Fat	3g	Sodium	12mg
228	Protein	1g	Carbohydrates	44g

Fruit Crisp

This dessert bakes up nicely in the microwave as well as the oven.

Prep Time: 10 min   Serves: 2
Cook Time: 1-5 min or 45 min

INGREDIENTS

about 2 cups diced or sliced fruit

2 tablespoons soft butter,
coconut oil, or vegetable oil

2 tablespoons brown sugar

4 tablespoons rolled oats

2 tablespoons whole wheat flour

½ teaspoon ground cinnamon

3 tablespoons chopped walnuts,
pecans or almonds, optional

DIRECTIONS

1. Place fruit in a microwave safe dish. Use a dish that is wide enough so that the fruit is about 1 inch deep in the bottom.

2. In a separate bowl, mix together butter/oil, oats, brown sugar, flour, cinnamon, and nuts.

3. Sprinkle the mixture over the fruit.

4. Microwave on high 1-5 minutes or until fruit is as tender as you like it. OR In a regular oven: Bake at 375° F for 45 minutes or until the top is golden brown.

TIPS

Frozen fruit works well in this recipe. Just be sure to thaw it before using. or you can use canned fruit that has been rinsed to remove the sugar.

Nutrition Facts *(using vegetable oil)*

Calories	Total Fat	15g	Dietary Fiber	6g
Per serving	Saturated Fat	<1g	Sodium	6mg
336	Protein	5g	Carbohydrates	48g

Healthy dinners made easy.

Visit EatFresh.org to stretch your CalFresh dollars.

Made in the USA
Monee, IL
11 October 2020